BRILLIANT BRITS
ELIZABETH I

RI

Which queen was nearly executed by her own sister?

Which queen had one of the first-ever WCs installed in her palace?

Which queen swore a lot and drank beer for breakfast?

Which queen beat the Armada and was 'the Mother of her Country'?

ELIZABETH I

Not another girl!

Elizabeth's father was Henry VIII, who was famous for having six wives. Her mother was his second wife, Anne Boleyn. Elizabeth was a disappointment. They'd both wanted a boy. When she was three, Henry had Anne's head chopped off because he thought she was cheating on him.

There's an old story that as a child Elizabeth fell ill and died. The people looking after her, terrified of Henry's anger, found a boy who looked just like her. Henry never noticed the difference, but the boy had to go on pretending, so Queen Elizabeth was really a man! It's nonsense.

Elizabeth had an older sister, Mary, who didn't like her much, and a younger brother, Edward, whom she loved. When she was eight her father chopped the head off his fifth wife, Katharine. Elizabeth swore then never to marry.

After Henry VIII died Edward became king. He was only nine. Elizabeth, who was thirteen, went to live with her last stepmother, also called Katharine, and her ten-year-old cousin Lady Jane Grey. Katharine was very kind.

LADY JANE   QUEEN KATHARINE   SEYMOUR   ELIZABETH   KAT   THOMAS

Living with them was Elizabeth's nurse, Kat, who had been with her since she was four, and her tutor Thomas. He was most unusual for those times, because he didn't beat his pupils. Elizabeth was a bit clever. She learnt to speak seven languages and her handwriting was excellent.

Things soon got complicated. Katharine married Edward's uncle, Admiral Seymour. Everybody thought he was fun, but one day Katharine found him kissing Elizabeth, so she sent Elizabeth away. Then Katharine died and Seymour hatched a plot to marry Elizabeth and make himself ruler of England. He was found out and executed.

A few years later, sadly, Edward died. And there was another plot to make Lady Jane Grey queen, instead of Mary who was next in line. Mary had Jane's head cut off. All this made Elizabeth very nervous.

England was a Protestant country, but Mary was a Catholic. Soon after she became queen there was a plot by Protestants to get rid of her. Elizabeth was a Protestant, but it had nothing to do with her. Even so Mary shut her in the Tower of London for a while. Elizabeth was terrified her head was next for the chop.

Mary married the King of Spain, and became very unpopular because she burnt a lot of Protestants. She tried to make Elizabeth marry a Catholic prince. Elizabeth said, 'I would rather die!' She was sent away to live in the country.

One cold November morning in 1558 Elizabeth was sitting under an oak tree at Hatfield Palace when she heard that Mary had died and she was queen.

BRRR! BRRR!

This is the Lord's doing: it is marvellous in our eyes.

With her was her trusted adviser William Cecil, and not long afterwards Robert Dudley rode up on a white horse. He had been a prisoner in the Tower while she was there. These two would become her closest friends.

Elizabeth was crowned in Westminster Abbey on a snowy January day. Afterwards she processed along a blue carpet to Westminster Hall. The people were so thrilled with their new queen that they tore the carpet to bits for souvenirs.

As queen, Elizabeth liked routine. After a brisk walk in her garden she drank beer for breakfast. Then she did her papers. After lunch she saw foreign visitors. She often kept them standing for hours, and insisted on speaking in Latin.

She loved riding and playing her lute on her barge. In the evenings dancing and banquets were followed by cards, at which she cheated. Then she would often keep her ministers up half the night discussing the running of the country.

Please God, send my mistress a husband!

At first Cecil didn't think a woman could run the country, but he soon realised how sensible and clever Elizabeth was. Even so he prayed every night that she would marry and have a son who could be king if anything happened to her.

As soon as Elizabeth became queen, foreign princes started sending her their portraits. The three most powerful countries in Europe were France, Spain and Austria. England needed an ally and the best way to get one was for her to marry a prince from one of these countries.

At first she said she might marry the King of Spain, then a couple of princes from Austria, and then a couple from France, not to mention princes from several other countries at the same time. Everybody was confused.

One poor prince, Eric of Sweden, twice set sail to ask for Elizabeth's hand, only to be shipwrecked both times. He sent his brother instead, but Elizabeth started flirting with the brother so Eric recalled him. An endless stream of portraits and love letters in Latin only stopped after Eric's brother murdered him.

The truth is that Elizabeth realised she could keep England from being invaded by playing off these foreign princes one against the other. She did really fancy the French Duke of Anjou, whom she nicknamed 'my Frog', and several Englishmen also thought they had a chance. In the end she never married anyone.

The one man Elizabeth really might have married was tall, dark and handsome Robert Dudley. She laughed with him, rode with him, danced with him every night, and even tickled his neck when she made him Earl of Leicester. All the other courtiers were extremely jealous.

But Leicester was already married. When his wife, Amy, died mysteriously by falling downstairs, everybody said he had murdered her. He was most likely innocent but Elizabeth couldn't risk marrying him after that. She just kept him dangling.

They often gave each other presents. He gave her the first wristwatch in history and she gave him a castle.

LEICESTER
Possible murderer, foolish, poor, unpopular, only one castle

CHARLES
Son of an emperor, sensible, rich, popular, lots of castles

William Cecil, now Lord Burghley, didn't approve of Leicester. He drew up a chart comparing him and Charles of Austria as possible husbands.

The King of Spain will send a great fleet and you will defeat it.

It was Leicester who introduced Elizabeth to a mysterious magician called Dr John Dee. Elizabeth became convinced that Dr Dee could tell the future.

Elizabeth had at least seventeen palaces around London. She hated smells and moved palace whenever one of them got stinky. Immediately the WC was invented in 1596, she had one installed at Richmond Palace.

WINDSOR CASTLE

KENILWORTH CASTLE
which she gave to Leicester.
She then invited herself to stay and
complained she couldn't see the garden
from her room, so he had it all
dug up and moved in the night.

Many of her subjects built their houses in the shape of an 'E' in her honour.

HAMPTON COURT

LORD LINCOLN'S HOUSE AT CHELSEA

Anybody home?

NONSUCH
her favourite palace

RICHMOND PALACE

RIVER THAMES

In summer she loved to travel around and visit her subjects, usually arriving with about five hundred people. It cost so much to have her to stay that Lord Lincoln locked his house and ran away. She simply came back the next week.

BURGHLEY HOUSE
It cost Lord Burghley £1000 to have Elizabeth to stay for 10 days ... several million in today's money.

HATFIELD PALACE
where she was told she was queen

QUEEN ELIZABETH'S HUNTING LODGE

LONDON
Elizabeth's main palace was WHITEHALL but she had at least six other palaces in the city.

TOWER OF LONDON
Bad memories!

GREENWICH PALACE

Elizabeth liked parties, and she was particularly fond of picnics.

It took Elizabeth two hours each morning to decide which of her 3000 dresses and which red wig to wear. Unlike her subjects, she was very clean. She had at least five baths a year. She ate lots of sweets to make her breath smell nice . . . except they rotted all her teeth . . . and her white makeup was full of poisonous arsenic.

She was too terrified to go to the dentist, and always had toothache. As she got older she hated people painting her with rotten teeth and wrinkles, so she had one really flattering portrait done, which every other painter had to copy.

She dressed to look magnificent, with so many jewels that people were amazed she could stand up under the weight. Everybody had to bow to her. The Earl of Oxford once farted while doing so. He immediately left court in shame and didn't dare return for seven years. When he did, Elizabeth started giggling.

She loved a good joke. She loved plays, especially funny ones, and she had the best . . . Shakespeare wrote plays for her. But she also had a bad temper. She threw things and even boxed Burghley's ears if she didn't like his advice.

Although they had never met, Elizabeth at first tried to be friends with her cousin Mary, Queen of Scots. But Catholic Mary thought she should be Queen of England as well as Scotland, instead of Protestant Elizabeth.

Mary made herself so unpopular in Scotland that she had to flee to England. Elizabeth knew that if she sent her back Mary might be put to death. But if she let her stay, it might encourage Catholics to plot to make Mary queen instead of her.

So Elizabeth kept Mary prisoner in various castles while she tried to decide what to do. It wasn't a very hard prison. Mary had about fifty servants and lots of pets. Even so she kept writing letters and plotting against Elizabeth.

Elizabeth's ministers spied on Mary until they found some letters which proved her plotting. They advised Elizabeth to have her head chopped off. Elizabeth hated the idea, but eventually she agreed.

Philip, the Catholic King of Spain, had supported Mary's wish to be Queen of England. He was furious with the English because of sailors such as Sir Francis Drake and Sir Walter Raleigh who attacked his ships and stole his treasure.

Elizabeth loved the stolen jewels Drake brought her. Raleigh brought tobacco and potatoes from America. Famously he once spread his cloak over a puddle so Elizabeth would not get her feet wet. Adventurers like these opened up the seas for trade and founded the colonies which became the British Empire.

Philip created a huge fleet known as the Armada to invade England. Drake, Raleigh and others organised the English fleet to fight it. Elizabeth made a famous speech.

When the Armada arrived in 1588 a terrible storm scattered the Spanish ships. Many were wrecked as the English ships chased them. Elizabeth was so excited at the victory that she is said to have ridden her horse up a flight of stairs.

Celebrations for the victory were ruined for Elizabeth by the death of Leicester soon afterwards. They were all getting old. She had not allowed Burghley to retire. By 1598 he was exhausted and he too died.

No prince in Europe hath such a counsellor.

He's turned his back on the Queen!!!

I want an army to command.

Go to the devil!

But she had one consolation. The Earl of Essex, Leicester's stepson, was tall and handsome. Although thirty years her junior and sometimes very rude to her, he became her new favourite. The thing he loved most was playing soldiers. He kept on and on at her to let him command her army.

Eventually Elizabeth let him take an army to Ireland, but he got bored and disobeyed her by riding back to London. He even barged into her bedroom while she was still dressing. Elizabeth was furious.

Next he plotted to take over the country by force so he didn't have to obey her at all any more. Burghley's son, Robert Cecil, found out and surrounded his house. Essex had to be persuaded down off the roof. After this Elizabeth agreed he must have his head chopped off, but she was so sad that she lost interest in life.

Elizabeth lived on for a year or so. Then for three weeks she refused to go to bed, fearing that if she did she would die. She was right. She died soon afterwards in bed, aged seventy. Her ring was dropped from the window to a horseman below who took it to her successor, James VI of Scotland, Mary's son.

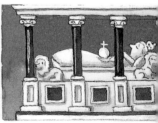

James ordered a magnificent tomb to be built in Westminster Abbey, describing her as 'the Mother of her Country'. For forty years she had kept England at peace and safe from invasion. Her sailors had explored the world. Shakespeare had written his plays. This was the great Elizabethan Age.